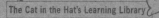

The Cat in the Hat's Learning Library

The Cat in the Hat's Learning Library

The Cat in the Hat's Learning Library

The Cat in the Hat's Learning Library

The Cat in the Hat's Learning Library

The Cat in the Hat's Learning Library

The Cat in the Hat's Learning Library
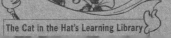

The Cat in the Hat's Learning Library

The Cat in the Hat's Learning Library

The Cat in the Hat's Learning Library

To all my friends at
Reach Out and Read, with love
—T.R.

The editors would like to thank
BARBARA KIEFER, Ph.D.,
Charlotte S. Huck Professor of Children's Literature,
The Ohio State University, and
JIM BREHENY,
Director, Bronx Zoo,
for their assistance in the preparation of this book.

TM & copyright © by Dr. Seuss Enterprises, L.P. 2016
THE CAT IN THE HAT'S LEARNING LIBRARY logos and word mark are registered trademarks of
Dr. Seuss Enterprises, L.P.
THE CAT IN THE HAT'S LEARNING LIBRARY logos © Dr. Seuss Enterprises, L.P. 1998

THE CAT IN THE HAT KNOWS A LOT ABOUT THAT! logo and word mark TM 2010 Dr. Seuss
Enterprises, L.P., Portfolio Entertainment, Inc., and Collingwood O'Hare Productions, Ltd.
All rights reserved. The PBS KIDS logo is a registered trademark of PBS. Both are used with
permission. All rights reserved.

Visit us on the Web!
Seussville.com
randomhousekids.com

Educators and librarians, for a variety of teaching tools, visit us at RHTeachersLibrarians.com

Library of Congress Cataloging-in-Publication Data
Rabe, Tish, author.
High? low? where did it go? : all about animal camouflage / by Tish Rabe ; illustrated by
Aristides Ruiz and Joe Mathieu.
    pages cm. — (The Cat in the Hat's learning library)
Summary: "The Cat in the Hat introduces young readers to the concept of camouflage—a type of
adaptation that helps animals survive." —Provided by publisher.
Audience: Ages 5–8.
ISBN 978-0-449-81496-3 (trade) — ISBN 978-0-375-97169-3 (lib. bdg.)
1. Camouflage (Biology)—Juvenile literature. 2. Protective coloration (Biology)—Juvenile
literature. 3. Animals—Color—Juvenile literature. 4. Animal behavior—Juvenile literature.
I. Ruiz, Aristides, ill. II. Mathieu, Joe, ill. III. Title. IV. Series: Cat in the Hat's learning library.
QL767.R33 2016 591.47'2—dc23 2015018390

Printed in the United States of America 10 9 8 7 6 5 4 3 2 1

High? Low? Where Did It Go?

by Tish Rabe

illustrated by Aristides Ruiz and Joe Mathieu

The Cat in the Hat's Learning Library®

Random House 🏠 New York

I'm the Cat in the Hat.
Come and travel with me
to find animals that
are not easy to see.

Camouflage helps them hide.
It's the way they're concealed,
but these hidden animals
will soon be revealed!

All over the world,
animals must adapt
to the conditions
of their habitat.

Adaptations are traits
that help animals survive—
different looks or behaviors
that keep them alive.

An example is camouflage,
which helps to protect them.
If they cannot be seen,
others may not detect them.

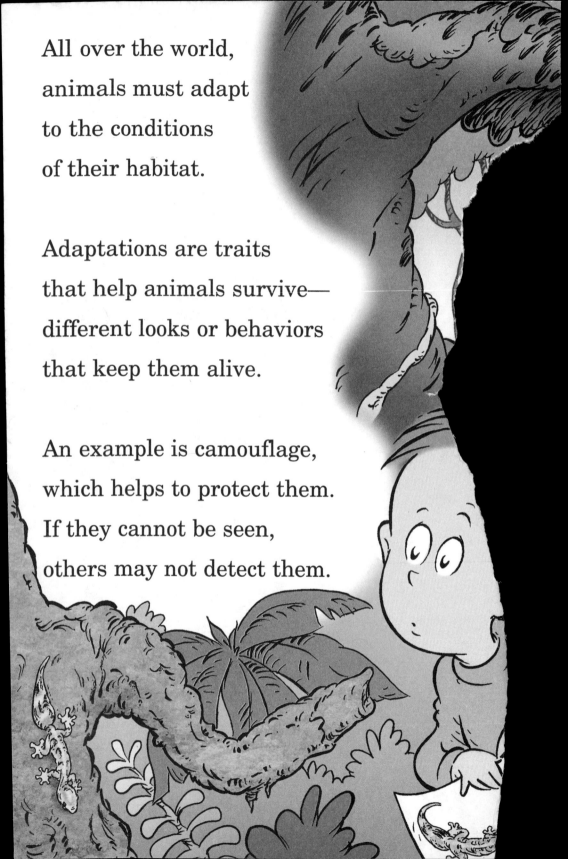

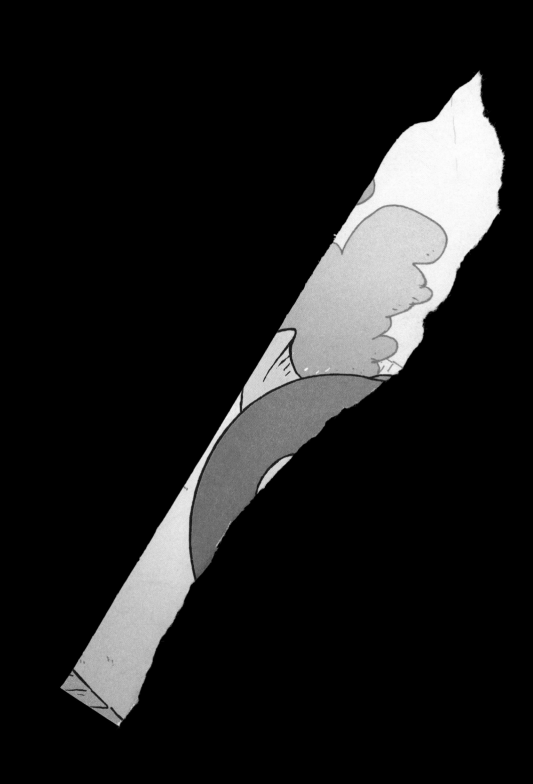

TURNIP-TAILED GECKO

There are different kinds
of camouflage adaptation.
This first one is called
concealing coloration.

Some animals change color
to match their background.
It helps them blend in
so they may not be found.

Concealing coloration
is a type of
camouflage.

During the winter,
this little stoat
blends in with the snow
with its fluffy white coat.

In the spring, it will grow
a new coat that is brown
so it can blend in with
colors on the ground.

This sloth barely moves.
When he does, he's so slow
that on his shaggy fur
some plants start to grow!

These plants are called algae.
They turn his fur green.
He blends in with the leaves
and can hardly be seen!

Some animals change color
when danger is near.
Predators may not
even know they are here.

These are flashlight fish.
Watch as they swim by.
They have glowing bacteria
under each eye.

These bacteria let out
a bright greenish glow,
which lights up dark water
wherever they go.

But when they're in danger,
small folds in their skin
cover the glow
so the fish can blend in.

Some animals hide
right in front of our eyes.
They are hard to see
'cause they wear a **disguise**!

To keep hidden, some look
just like things they are not.
It's the reason why
they're not easy to spot.

This leafy sea dragon
floats in the ocean.
It looks like seaweed
as it moves in slow motion.

LEAFY SEA
DRAGON

This violet snail
can hide easily.
It makes bubbles and looks
just like foam on the sea.

This flounder looks just like
the rocky seabed.
We see only its eyes
on the side of its head.

Scuba dive in the ocean,
and you may get a shock!
The poisonous stonefish
looks just like a rock!

The insect on this tree
has a life-saving trick.
Instead of an insect,
it looks like a stick!

WALKING STICK

Sticks do not run, so
when threatened, it will
stop where it is
and then stay very still.

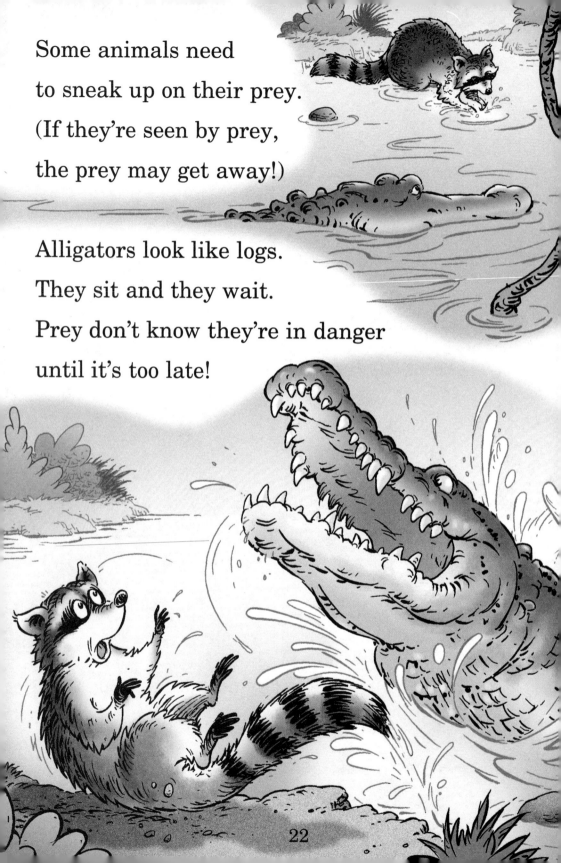

Some animals need
to sneak up on their prey.
(If they're seen by prey,
the prey may get away!)

Alligators look like logs.
They sit and they wait.
Prey don't know they're in danger
until it's too late!

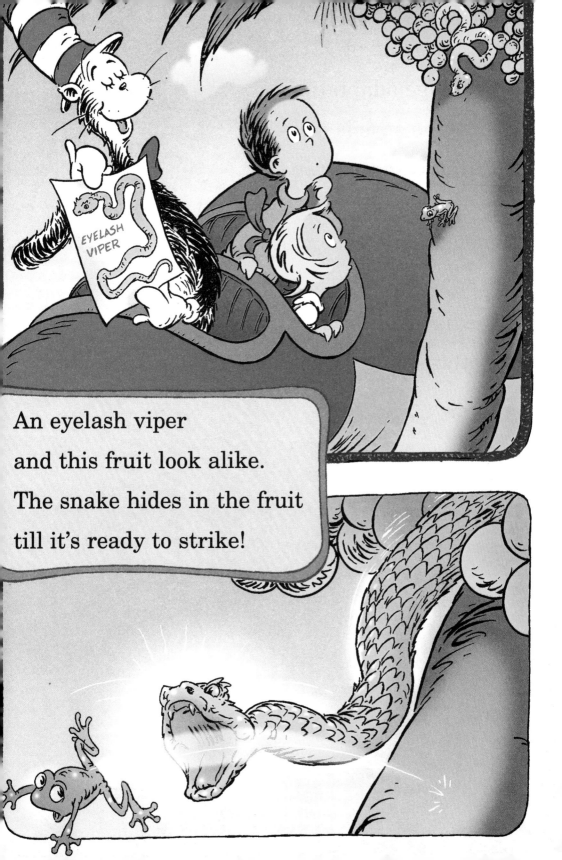

An eyelash viper
and this fruit look alike.
The snake hides in the fruit
till it's ready to strike!

EYELASH
VIPER

This next kind of
camouflage adaptation
Thing One says is called
disruptive coloration.

Some animals have markings
like stripes, patches, and dots.
Some have a few markings,
but others have lots.

DISRUPTIVE
COLORATION
IS A
TYPE OF
CAMOUFLAGE.

Markings help hide their shape.
Is this tiger big or small?
Its stripes hide it so we
can't see its shape at all.

This little fawn has
white dots on her fur.
In a field of white flowers,
it's hard to see her.

While mother finds food,

she leaves her fawn behind.

The fawn's markings protect her.

She's not easy to find.

A bittern's feathers are striped
and that's what it needs,
to keep undercover and
hide in the reeds.

When wind hits the reeds,
the bird sways side to side.
Its stripes look like the reeds,
and that helps it to hide.

BITTERN

A lion moves in
but can't tell them apart.
Where does mother end?
Where does baby start?

To stay safe, some animals
use this survival trick—
they **mimic** other animals
that make predators sick.

A bird gets sick if it eats
a monarch butterfly,
so it won't try to catch one.
It lets monarchs fly by.

They spend their whole lives trying to disappear. Can you find ten of them? They are hiding right here!

Answer on page 45

GLOSSARY

Adaptation: A change of form or behavior to survive in different surroundings.

Algae: Tiny plant without roots, stems, or leaves.

Camouflage: The hiding of things so they cannot be seen or recognized easily.

Conceal: To hide or cover from sight.

Countershading: A form of camouflage in which some parts of an animal's body are dark and some are light.

Disguise: To change appearance in order to hide.

Disruptive: Causing separation or division into different parts.

Habitat: The place where a person or thing is usually found.

Mimic: To copy or be like something else.

Predator: An animal that lives by capturing and eating other animals.

Prey: An animal that is hunted by other animals for food.

Reveal: To uncover or allow to be seen.

Scuba: Equipment worn by divers for breathing underwater.

Trait: A distinct or different feature or quality.

FOR FURTHER READING

101 Hidden Animals by Melvin and Gilda Berger (Scholastic). Fun facts and photos of amazing camouflaged animals. For grades two and up.

How to Hide an Octopus and Other Sea Creatures by Ruth Heller (Grosset & Dunlap, *Reading Railroad Books*). Realistic illustrations and simple, rhyming text introduce young readers to camouflaged sea creatures. Other books in the series include *How to Hide a Butterfly and Other Insects* and *How to Hide a Crocodile and Other Reptiles*. For preschool and up.

What Color Is Camouflage? by Carolyn Otto, illustrated by Megan Lloyd (HarperTrophy, *Let's-Read-and-Find-Out Science®*, Stage 2). A simple introduction to how and why different animals use camouflage. For kindergarten and up.

Where in the Wild? Camouflaged Creatures Concealed . . . and Revealed by David M. Schwartz and Yael Schy, with photographs by Dwight Kuhn (Tricycle Press). This unique book, an NSTA-CBC Outstanding Science Trade Book for Children, combines artful photographs of camouflaged animals with poems that give clues to their identities. For preschool and up.

INDEX

Camouflaged animals play hide-and-seek day and night. To survive and find food, they must stay out of sight.

They spend their whole lives trying to disappear. Can you find ten of them? They are hiding right here!

The Cat in the Hat's Learning Library

The Cat in the Hat's Learning Library

The Cat in the Hat's Learning Libra

The Cat in the Hat's Learning Library

The Cat in the Hat's Learning Library

The Cat in the Hat's Learning Libra

The Cat in the Hat's Learning Library

The Cat in the Hat's Learning Library

The Cat in the Hat's Learning Libra

The Cat in the Hat's Learning Library

The Cat in the Hat's Learning Library

The Cat in the Hat's Learning Libra

The Cat in the Hat's Learning Library

The Cat in the Hat's Learning Library

The Cat in the Hat's Learning Libra

The Cat in the Hat's Learning Library®